Catnip, Toilet Paper, and Lasers

Copyright © 2020 by MGSpear

All rights reserved.

Names, characters, institutions, and events are either the product of the author's imagination or experience, used fictitiously, or used with permission.

I'd like to thank my husband who let me read him cat poetry many days after getting off work.

Also a big thank you to everyone who shared their cat stories with me and believed in this project.

Introduction: Read first

In this collection you will be introduced to many different cats: my two pretties, Socks and Elsa, a handful of others, and many unnamed cats. When you see the **, this will signal the end of a poem and that cat's point of view. Each poem starts fresh with a different story from a different cat perspective.

What is the answer?

What will prevail?

Will it be the red dot?

Or will the cat win the tale?

Socks

My name is Socks,

and much to my delight,

I chase a red dot

almost every single night.

It travels over bed sheets

and runs across the floor

while I chase to my heart's content

thirsting for more!

By day I sleep;

by night I chase

when my human comes home from work

and pulls out the laser post-haste!

I hear the clicking of the button

and race into the room

to run after that red dot--

look at me zoom! **

My name is Elsa
and my human leaves cups
for me to lick the bottom
to perform my own cleanups!

Sometimes it's milk
other times it's water,
but either way I am close by
like a determined squatter.

Then he goes to bed
and I make my move
my tongue goes to work
as I get in the groove.

I lick it clean
careful not to tip over;
sometimes Socks joins
and he tries a takeover!

I am the cup cleaner

that is my tale

my human suspects

though I have never yet failed. **

My name is Tiger
and I'm adventurous and bold
I am better than a guard dog
or so I have been told.

When not protecting family
I get leash walked outside
where I meet many a grasshopper
which I play with and hide.

Other sunny days
I sit in a chair
and bask in the sun
without so much a care.

To the mailbox is nice,
exploring pasture more fun;
I will go on walks anywhere
as long as in the sun. **

Presents are fun
to slink in and hide;
the tissue paper hugs me
all colored and tie-dyed.

I poke my head out
mewing for all to see;
I am the cutest cat around
please look at me!

The paper crinkles and tears
while I have fun in the sack,
then my human pulls me out
giving me much flack.

But always I return
looking for crinkling paper
I burrow into the tissue
ready for my next peek-a-boo caper. **

My name is Annie
and I'm as colorful as they come;
hues litter my fur
bringing jealousy from some.

My fur does get dirty
since I play outside
and go on adventures
with a coat that's tie-dyed.

I am a country cat
the fields are where I prowl;
sometimes I see cool things
or smell stuff very foul.

But always I return home
and get petted all the time
I am adored by all who see me
even if covered in grime. **

Socks:

I pounce and toss catnip mice

while running around to play;

I could sling them up in the air

and be content all day.

Sometimes I rub my face in them

feeling the softness of their fur

I await what comes next

as I start to purr.

You see I tend to shred the mice

on the couch where I lay

and dump all the catnip

into the cushions as I play.

Now whenever I want to feel good

I go sit on that couch

breathing in the smell of catnip

like a contented slouch. **

My owner bathes sometimes
and I worry they might drown
humans aren't made for swimming;
I'd be devastated if they went down.

So I jump up on the ledge
to oversee the bath;
one time I got hyper
and fell off my path.

Into the water I went
with a loud pop and splash
my fur got all wet;
I was out in a flash.

Still I watch them bathe
making sure things go right
so they don't slip under
and give me a fright. **

My name is Hobbes
I could catch mice all day
as they run through the house
grabbing them to play.

First I sling the mice around
then lug them along;
I mew in delight
this is my song.

I wash them in water
my prey that I found;
they slosh in a circle
making funny swooshy sounds.

Then I take the cleaned prey
to where my humans will see
so they can praise my awesome skills
and notice the mice no longer flee. **

I like to fly through the air

as my human launches me

body streamlined for precision

while he looks on with glee.

On bed sheets I land

where my human pets me;

turning I mew for more--

I fly better than a bee.

I wait for him to come home

as we do this every night

where I fly like wings carry me;

my joy shines ever so bright.

Some think my passion is weird

to wish to fly like a bird

but I've always been told to chase your dreams--

what have you heard? **

Elsa:

They got us a new cat tree!

One huge array of sits,

with boxes and scratching posts as well--

it was a set of kits.

We first play with the boxes

as they are being built

then sniff out the scratching posts;

occasionally screws are spilt.

Our humans figure it out

and up it goes

towering over the desk

towards the top of the windows.

Then we jump up and explore

checking things out as we play;

we are the monarchs of this house

declare it everyone, I say! **

My human got a costume
of which she made me wear;
I now look like a pumpkin
of course I throw a glare.

She pulls out more attire
taking out next a hat
now I look like a witchy pumpkin;
this time I spat.

Then she adds butterfly wings
to my pumpkin flair;
now I look like a pumpkin fairy--
this is more than I can bear.

We then sit on the front porch
and begin to pass out candy;
everyone comes up to pet me--
maybe this costume came in handy. **

My human had a string
sticking out of her cup
I sat near watching intently
as she lifted the cup up.

That string still dangled out
tempting me much more
I stalked closer towards the drink
from the living room floor.

She sipped a few more times
then picked up her phone
yet the cup stayed in hand;
I think my cover is blown.

But wait!

Down it goes
until it's set on the table;
I snag that tea string
as soon as I am able. **

I sit on the mini-fridge
to snooze the afternoon away
stretching out in my sleep
I sometimes rock and sway.

My bed is in the other room
but I prefer this spot
my human calls me picky
but I am not fraught.

Sunlight comes through the window
to shine down on me
I stretch as I get warm--
this is the better place you see.

But once I stretched too much
and rolled over the edge
I landed between the shoes--
they made a type of wedge.

I couldn't get out
and mewed for assistance;
my human heard those cries
and went the distance.

She put me back on the frig
where I purred my delight
and relaxed in the sunshine
as I got over my plight. **

Elsa:

One night I jumped on the stove

to lick the soup bowl

making loud slurping sounds

as the food made me whole.

Then kitchen lights turn on

as I continue eating

licking as much as possible

this delicious treat so fleeting.

My human walks in

and sees me on the stove

he yells to get off

so I stopped licking and dove.

But while jumping down

I knock off the ladle;

it smacks my human's face,

taking flight from its cradle.

He cleans up the mess

as I lick soup off the floor

then grumbling goes to bed

saying no more, no more. **

My name is Sam
and I love to go outside;
I launch at the screen door
energetic and wide-eyed.

Outside the birds fly
and grasshoppers leap;
squirrels run around the trees--
this is not the time to sleep.

Once the patio door opened
but the screen was left in place
I leaped forward without realizing
and bounced backwards post-haste.

My goal was still the same
I mewed to be let outside;
finally the screen door opened
I ran through--what a ride! **

Outside I sit in a tree
to watch and look for prey;
sometimes though I nap instead
and sleep away the day.

Once a creature climbed my tree--
it was another cat--
he jumped up to hiss at me,
then we got into a spat.

I swatted with my paws,
he swatted back at me;
it was a battle of the ages
for my favorite tree.

Soon I knocked him off
and he tumbled to the ground
yowling at me pathetically;
my human came out to the sound.

He told me I was bad
so I swatted at his hair
then I fell also to the ground--
this so isn't fair.

But my claws still entangled
pulled my human down too;
now we're both in the grass--
I didn't get treats later to chew. **

I lick when I'm hungry;
I lick when I'm not;
I lick when I'm in the mood--
my love is not bought.

I spread cheer freely
with the wetness of my tongue
and will lick anytime
the old and the young.

I tend to lick at random times
when people try to pet me;
my tongue licks rapidly
while kids squeal with glee.

My humans think I lick too much
and keep me a bay
but then I jump into their laps
they really have no say. **

I run all over

during the day

not coming to calls;

my human and I play keep-away.

I zoom around

burrowing into covers

sitting very still

while nearby my human hovers.

But when night falls

the air gets chilly

and I begin to wonder

maybe I'm acting silly.

So I jump on the bed

to sleep near my owner

taking in their body heat;

I'm not truly a loner. **

My name is Callie
and when I was little
I was dumped at a house
all terrified and brittle.

A man picked me up
I snuggled in his chest;
he consulted with his wife
that I would be their guest.

I played outside
but birds tried to get me
so I hid in a truck;
now the birds couldn't see.

Then the truck started up
on an adventure I went;
I was discovered at the market
all tired and spent.

The man was not mad

and took me back home;

I'm now very happy--

through their house I roam. **

Most cats mew
or chirp or hiss
but I quack like a duck;
I don't think I'm amiss.

People laugh and pet me
exclaiming I'm just so cute;
they want me to quack more;
I am never on mute.

One person met me
and didn't believe my sound
until I quacked for her a lot
then she petted me all around.

My human thinks it's cute
that my quack brings such laughter;
people stay and buy things
and then laugh some more after. **

Elsa:

I pass the day away
laying on my cat tree
sprawled out across the top;
it's really all about me.

Sometimes my brother joins
and gets angry I am fat;
there's just more of me to go around
to love and to pat.

Still he gets upset
when he can't sun himself,
so he jumps nearby
and sits on the high dresser shelf.

There we both lay
bathing in the sun;
our humans calls us lazy,
but we're just having fun. **

My name is Fatty
and I'm great at finding things
I'll stare down all escapees
even things with wings.

One time a snake got out
my slumber was disturbed
to seek out the reptile--
I wasn't a bit perturbed.

Within twenty minutes
I found it and stared
at a closet with drawers
all closed and squared.

My human came over
and searched through the drawers;
she found the elusive snake--
this is one of my favorite chores. **

One week the leaves fell
all over the grass
I watched through a window--
my moment at last.

My human raked leaves
this way and that,
gathering up in a pile
then tapping it flat.

I saw my chance
and zoomed out the door
aiming straight for the pile--
this will be a great score.

Jumping into the leaves
I land with a splat;
my human isn't happy
but still gives me a pat. **

I dig in the trash
for tasty treats
pushing aside vegetables
just going for the meats.

I do this at night
so my humans don't see;
if they happen to wake up
that's my cue to flee.

Sometimes I find steak,
other times fish;
my humans eat all kinds of meat
but never share their dish.

So I took to the trash,
except last night I was caught
now the trash is outside
and I am distraught. **

One time we decided
the carpet was up for grabs;
we tore a section all to pieces,
claws doing damaging stabs.

Our humans came home
and much to their horror
they saw our handiwork
in the master bedroom corner.

This lead to a re-flooring
in all of the rooms;
boxes piled everywhere--
such fun ahead looms!

It took a whole year
to get everything done;
those boxes were awesome
until there were none. **

My human was sleeping

on her soft bed

then I got the notion

to sit on her head.

In the morning she woke

but I had already left;

I timed to opening eyes--

yes I am quite deft.

She claimed trouble breathing

of this I didn't care--

her head was my pillow,

feet entangled in hair.

Then she set up a recording

to monitor sleep;

it caught me coming up

doing my midnight creep.

She saw I lay on her face

practically every night;

now the bedroom door stays shut

as I am kept out of sight. **

I play with my ball
it makes a jingly sound;
my human gets irritated
taking it away as I frown.

I attack his pant leg
using my claws
they get stuck in the fabric--
he unhooks my paws.

I demand my ball back
with many a mew;
this seems so unfair--
justice is askew.

Then I found where he hid it
and when timing's just right
I will chase across the floor
every minute of the night. **

I have fun with my toys
until they disappear;
they roll under the dresser
lost forever I fear.

My human gets me new ones
and they disappear too;
it seems there is a black abyss
where all my toys shoo.

Then my human got a stick
and shoved it underneath
they all came rolling out!
I tackle with my teeth.

My human grabbed some
throwing toys on the bed;
jumping up I snag a ball.
"You're a pretty kitty," she said. **

When I was younger
and ever so small
I wished to jump on cabinets;
alas they were too tall.

Then I got bigger
and stronger too
I was able to jump up
having adventures anew.

I walked on those cabinets
the frig as well,
then found some secret places--
of these I won't tell.

Then my humans came home
and saw me up top;
they demanded I get down
telling me to stop.

But when they're not around

on adventures I go

wherever I want

just going with the flow. **

Elsa:

We got an automated litter box
of which I did not care
though interesting to watch it clean;
I'd sit in front and stare.

They set it for two cats
to go off twice day
we jumped in between cleanings;
this was the way.

Until came a time
when I really had to go
but it was in a cleaning
so that was a no.

I jumped into a basket
as my bladder would not wait
and peed until empty
in my temporary crate.

The humans were not happy
but hey I had to go;
a second litter box was added
to escape another tale of woe…

for now. **

I lay on my back
inviting people to pet me
I am cute, cuddly, and pretty
for everyone to see.

Then when they reach down
I arch up to bite
like a touch-me-not flower
I am only a precious sight.

I love to bite hands
and scratch skin as well
there is no greater joy--
if you know of one, do tell. **

My name is Stella
and I am a dancer
when the music comes on
I should be called Prancer.

I jump into the air
twisting around
my tail flicks like crazy--
no one has a frown.

My human starts laughing
her kids join in too
as I jump and twist
like a bouncy corkscrew.

Then the music stops
and my dancing ceases
but my human was so amused
she gives me cat chew pieces. **

I wonder what they will do;
I wonder what they'll say;
you see I'm hiding in the towel rack
tensed and ready to play.

Someone comes into the bathroom
starting up the shower;
soon they will reach for a towel
then I will have the power.

Instead I get anxious
and stick my head out
in between towels;
my intentions I flout.

My human laughs at me
and says I'm really cute;
she scratches my head
telling me I'm a hoot.

So now the routine is

when they take a shower

I hide in the towel rack

sticking my head out like a flower. **

I love cleaning day
when fresh litter is added
the poo box smells better--
it's definitely more padded.

When my human is done
I flop onto the litter
to roll in its freshness
like a good little critter.

I do kick some out
making a mess everywhere;
but hey it's my bathroom--
I don't really care.

My human sighs
scratching me anyway
then tries to coax me out;
thanks no I'll just stay. **

The clothes tumble in the dryer
and peak my attention
I'm a very observant kitty--
just thought I would mention.

Then I get curious
so when the clothes stop
I jump in quickly
with a nice little plop.

The clothes are so warm!
I've found my new bed
but my human doesn't agree
though she scratches my head.

I am shooed out
soon the clothes are gone too
but they're carried to the bedroom--
I'll be there in a few. **

Elsa:

A monkey is my favorite toy--
I stole it off the chair
and drag it all over
as it is my flair.

I growl when Socks comes
he steals it sometimes
and runs away with it
not atoning for his crimes.

So I steal it back
and we play tug-of-war
flopping that monkey
all over the floor.

It had a quaint little bell
that jingled all hours
and entertained me so much;
better than chewing on flowers.

Then my human took it
so it wouldn't chime at night
since then its not been seen
my once toy delight. **

My name is Loki
I swear I'm not askew
but I jump into my humans' pants
while they're taking a poo.

The fabric is nice and warm
as I snuggle in glee;
my human reaches to pet me
and I do not flee.

This is our special time
in which we bond together
they sit back and check their phone
looking at the weather.

We stay like this quite a while
all snuggled and warm;
I twist and turn in the pants--
this is truly an art form. **

In my human's study

there's a large swivel chair

that I love to jump on

and cover with my hair.

She sits typing

looking all intense,

I think she needs a break--

that's just my two cents.

So I jump on the chair

and climb to the top

where I lean against her head;

she doesn't say to stop.

I sit while she works

with occasional scratches

this makes me happy

and I don't claw the chair patches.

Then I got bored
and pushed more on her head
entangling my claws--
"Stop it," she said.

What I didn't know:
she's in a meeting;
I mew to virtual people
giving them my greeting. **

I love organizing:
when they get ready to arrange
their knickknacks and discards;
I wait for this change.

You see they bring out boxes
for storing things away;
I jump in and out
to delightfully play.

I sit in a box
while they fill it up
overflowing with trinkets
like a full brim teacup.

Then I jump out
and into the next
until it's filled up
then that box is hexed.

This goes on and on

until the last box--

it's filled with comfort;

I stay on this bed of socks. **

My name is Marlin
and I'm a nervous cat
I hide under the bed;
I am not one to chat.

I flee at any sound
leaving pee across the floor;
I head for safety all the time
zooming through the bedroom door.

When I feel safe
near my human I will sleep,
dreaming of a tranquil world;
of this I drink deep.

I wish I was brave
and strong with no fear
but alas my nervous temperament
does not bring much cheer. **

My human takes me places
traveling in his jeep;
it's usually a bumpy ride
but I don't make a peep.

We travel to the lake
and hike down the trails
having a great time--
this never fails.

I climb on rocks
and once crossed a stream;
we look out for each other--
we're a great team. **

When it gets cold
we snuggle together
my brothers and sisters
keeping warm in the weather.

Big sis lays on bottom
then we all pile on
and burrow into each other
sleeping 'til dawn.

We take shelter in the barn
where it's mostly nice and warm
sometimes hiding in the hay
safe from insect swarm.

On nights it rains
we listen to the thunder
then cuddle up together
and begin to slumber.

My family is big

and really nice too

I love our nights entwined;

we stick together like glue. **

My name is Lilo
and I like sugary sweets;
I stalk through the kitchen
looking for tasty treats.

Once there was a box
on top of the table;
I wait for them to leave
jumping up when able.

The contents smelled sweet
so I began to chew
a hole through the box
my how the time flew.

Soon I was in
and much to my delight
I feasted on donuts--
my glazed whiskers a sight! **

My thing is hunting socks
to carry through the house
they are always around
unlike my toy mouse.

So I take them everywhere
to drop where I please;
my humans shake their heads--
they think I'm a tease.

Plop! near the toilet.
Plop! on the rug.
Plop! on the bedroom floor
to cover up the bug.

I even take from baskets
when they are fresh and warm
and plop wherever I please--
this is the new norm. **

Elsa:

Magnets are flashy

catching my eye;

I watch them closely

like a cute little spy.

When no one looks

I creep forward to paw

down fall the magnets

with a sharp little claw.

My human walks in

when they're all on the floor

making a hissing sound

like that will settle the score.

Up go back the magnets

much to my delight

to knock down once again

when the timing's just right. **

The battle is on!
It's the vacuum versus me;
a showdown for the ages--
a sight for all to see.

It zooms over floors
and I attack with force
then realize it keeps going
unless I find the source.

Like a smart little kitty
I follow the black snake
until it reaches the wall;
this will be cake.

I grab hold with my teeth
and pull on the plug
then that vacuum dies--
now I am so smug. **

My name is Cassie
and my human has a fear:
she freaks out when spiders
begin to get near.

One night there was one
wrapped up in the sheet
she woke up screaming;
I watched ever so discreet.

I felt bad for my human
being freaked out
so I did something
to bring me some clout.

I bring a rubber spider
used for holidays
and mewed she was safe;
wow did I get praise. **

I like to scratch the couch
though my cat tree is near;
my humans run into the room
every time they hear.

They scold me
and tell me to stop
but I just stare at them
and start at the top.

Raking my claws
they come over to yell;
this happens like clockwork
like they're on a bell.

I switch to my tree
as they come near
they pet me all over
and call me a dear.

The jokes on them though

I have them trained

to come bring pets

with faces so pained. **

There once was a picture
that looked good enough to eat;
it was supposed to be a present
but I saw a tasty treat.

She tucked it away
from my prying paws
but I dragged it out
digging in with my claws.

I ripped off the wrapping
and chewed on the frame
if others tasted this good
I would have done the same.

She walks in
as I haul across the floor
but she takes it away
now I'm a little sore. **

Elsa:

I go where I'm forbidden,

licking dishes in the sink,

my tongue savors flavors

then I am gone in a blink.

Occasionally I get caught

and scamper to the couch

where I wait until it's clear

as I sit in a crouch.

Whenever I can

I feast to heart's delight

until they wash dishes

which feels like quite a slight.

So I wait until they eat

and fill the sink once more

then my hours are filled with licking--

I love this neglected chore. **

The bread looked so inviting,
a great place to hide;
the bag had a twist wrap
to keep sealed and tied.

I rip through the plastic
burrowing into the bread
there's nothing sticking out
except part of my head.

My human walks in
to grab a slice to eat
she jumps in surprise
at her mewing treat.

She starts to scold me
for covering it in hair
then tips me off the counter
which I don't think is fair. **

My name is Onyx
and I love to cuddle
I tackle my human;
on her chest I will huddle.

My purr box is fierce
as we cuddle for hours;
I comfort with sound
behold my cat powers!

I do hold grudges
and sometimes ignore.
When husband calls though
I stop being a bore.

But I am fiercely loyal
and will cuddle all night
even though I hold grudges
soon everything is alright. **

The food got left out
now it's time for play
rolling meatballs on the floor--
I will get my way.

I leave behind a trail
of tasty red sauce
as meatballs roll around--
I will teach them who's boss.

I sink my fangs
into one fleshy hide
carrying it to the bedroom
beaming with pride.

I plop it on the covers
mewing humans awake
they take my meatballs away--
how I miss them, how I ache. **

I get along with everyone
but the other cats do not;
they stay in separate spaces
like a savage breakup plot.

Since I like everyone
I get to visit both;
then bells were set up for me--
I love this new growth.

I ring the bell when I want in
and visit for a while
then I ring again to be let out
walking through with style.

Visiting around the house
I go where I may please;
sometimes though I ring the bell
just to be a tease. **

When I was a kitten
I snuck in small spaces
to nap the day away--
those were the best places.

My brother would join
snoozing in the dark
waking for nothing
dreaming of catching larks.

Then I got bigger
those small spaces grew tight;
once I got stuck
now that was a sight.

Half of me in,
half of me out;
I mewed for help,
wriggling with doubt.

My human walked over

and laughed at me

then pulled me loose;

now small spaces I flee. **

Slumbering on the couch
wrapped in covers
I hear my human calling;
nearby he hovers.

But I'm busy catching Z's
and don't want to be disturbed
so I ignore those calls;
now my human sounds perturbed.

He says my name again
shaking a treat box
but until the good stuff comes
there will be no talks.

Then I hear a can open
and smell the wet food;
I squirm out from hiding--
now I'm in the mood. **

I love canoe rides,
drifting over water,
it's so calm and peaceful--
oh look an otter!

The critter is in reach
now all I have to do
is stretch out with my claws--
it will have no clue.

But it moves while swatting
so I pout in the boat;
the otter chatters its teeth
as if talking to gloat.

Check it out! There's a fish--
scales flashing in the sun.
I reach out of the canoe
ready to have some fun.

But I lean out too far
falling into the blue
my human pulls me back
and laughs as I mew. **

Grasshoppers are
a delight to chase;
they hop through the grass
really all over the place.

There's one on a flower
so I begin to stalk;
it senses my movements;
I turn still as a rock.

Before it takes flight
I do a small little bounce
gathering my strength
then start to pounce.

My paws snag that insect
pinning to the ground;
it chirped to be let go--
what a funny little sound.

I carried it inside

jumping onto the couch;

my chase continues in cushions--

I am no slouch. **

Elsa:

The litter boxes worked fine

until one day I couldn't fit--

I tried to turn around and squat

but there wasn't room to sit.

You see the roof was too confining

the sides too close and small

I really tried to use them

but the coverings needed to fall.

So I found the next best thing

another empty basket;

I pissed to my heart's content

like a hose blowing a gasket.

My human came home

and found the mess

then rearranged the litter tops

like a game of chess.

Now I fit again

while taking my pisses

for now I am happy--

I give out kisses. **

My human has a hot tub
the heat is nice and warm
I always sit on the ledge
unless there is a storm.

I soak in all the heat
sprawling near the water
but one day I fell in
and got even hotter.

I mewed for help
as the heat pulled me down;
my feet paddling fast--
I thought I might drown.

Then paws touched bottom
and I reached for the ledge,
jumping out of the water--
now I don't sit near the edge. **

Socks:

We wrestle and we roll
all over the floor,
playfully biting ears
and nipping for more.

I am small
while my sister is bigger;
sometimes I chew her tail--
this is usually the trigger.

We jump into a box
intertwined with each other;
my sister uses her weight
trying to smother.

I wriggle around
to twist away
then swat her face
keeping up the play.

Soon she tires

stopping her attacks;

I calm down too

and we both relax. **

My human plays chess

off in the corner

starting at the pieces

like a sad mourner.

He doesn't play others,

just sits there every day;

I don't think it's relaxing--

there must be another way.

One day he stares intently

while I come up with a plan;

I sit innocent on the table;

the perfect con man.

He makes a move

I swat the knight from his hand

then knock off all the pieces;

on the floor they land.

And now I am banned from jumping on the table :(
**

Hair ties are the best
ask anyone around;
better than the jingly balls
that roll on the ground.

I carry them always
even if full of hair;
I bring them to my soft bed
and deposit in my lair.

My human wondered where they went
searching for missing ones
then saw my filled bed--
it was covered in tons.

Now she buys extra
so I keep my ties
and play until tired--
they are my prize. **

I have a secret
about a delicious treat;
I lick and bite lovingly--
they are ever so sweet.

My human gets mad
when I start doing my thing
but I go ahead anyway
because I am the king.

My treats I adore
are my human's toes
which I play with every night;
in his sleep they pose.

I tend to wake him up
as I lick my treats;
he tries to push me off
and toss me from the sheets.

Yet I come back
for a great time;
I must have toes--
this is my crime. **

I know where stuffed toys are:
with the sleeping child;
I sneak in to grab some
then run away wild.

I sling them about
and hide in random places;
only when she treats me well
does she end up in good graces.

I lead to the toys;
she smiles with delight
then blows me some kisses--
the parents love this sight.

This is how I train her
as she grows tall;
teaching respect for my tail
and for creatures great and small. **

Socks:

Boxes are my comfort zone
to sleep in and to hide
but when they're thrown away
I lay down teary-eyed.

But when they are there
they bring me delight
I tear open sides
reaching through to smite.

My claws grab feet
and Elsa too;
I reach my paw out
pulling stuff in for a chew.

Other times I nap
and slumber with dreams
of being a big kitty
jumping over large streams.

I love my boxes

they are so inviting

won't you come play--

that would be exciting! **

I knocked around
my human's cell phone
and it flashed at me;
my cover was blown.

So I slap some more,
pushing off the table,
then scoot under the couch
as soon as I was able.

She came into the room
looking for it;
I smiled
amazed at my wit.

Of course she found it
then the phone alerted her:
pictures of my deed;
it had close ups of my fur. **

I have a great hiding spot
that makes me look like a ghost
my black fur is made white--
I am the best hider I boast.

I can hide for hours
or even most of the day
then come out at night
cleaning myself before I play.

But she found my spot
by baking one day:
seeing me in the flour;
now the sack is kept at bay. **

My name is Nico
and I sleep in a can;
the metal feels warm--
I am a big fan.

While my humans sleep
in a fluffy bed
I prefer the can;
there is nothing to dread.

Everyone thinks it's weird
that I sleep in this place;
they don't know what they're missing--
this trash can is ace. **

The warmest spot in the house,

on the computer box,

radiates so much heat--

much better than warm socks.

I lay as my human works

typing the day away;

sometimes she sits for hours

while I just soak up warmth and stay.

One day I got bored

sprawled out on the top

I saw a black snake attached

and wondered where it stopped.

I pushed with my paws

twisting it around;

the black snake came off

and fell to the ground.

My human started cursing
getting very mad--
she lost all her unsaved work;
eh, I'm only a little sad. **

There once was a coke can
looking innocent and sweet
but it sat on my table--
this I must defeat.

My human hissed
for me to go away
but I kept coming on the table;
when he left it made my day.

I knocked that can clean off
it clattered to the floor
making a loud popping sound;
I was shaken to my core.

It sprayed everywhere
spewing this way and that;
my human was upset with me--
he called me a brat. **

Elsa:

Toilet paper is the best
to shred and to tear,
running through the house
with no one around to care.

Until my human comes home
and sees my décor
scattered in different places
all across the floor.

He yells my name
as I dash across the room
with a full roll in my mouth;
he chases me as I zoom.

Now the bathroom door stays shut
much to my despair;
I cry for my toilet paper--
I need to shred and tear! **

This year for Halloween
I was dressed as a spider;
no other costumes would fit
'cause I had gotten wider.

It had spindly little legs
that came off the sides;
they moved up and down
like the ocean tides.

She said I was cute
so we went on a walk;
instead of kids laughing
they started to gawk.

People thought my human
walked a spider tonight;
down the sidewalks we strolled
as kids whispered, "What a sight!"

I did scare the young ones

as I trotted along

but hey it's Halloween--

I definitely belong. **

My human ignores me
as he works from home;
I demand he pay attention
but alas he's in the zone.

I jump up on his keyboard
flopping my pretty self down
then he starts freaking out
I think acting like a clown.

He immediately pulls me off
into his lap
to show me jumbled messages--
Wow! Oh snap!

Those messages got sent
into his virtual meeting;
they all wanted to see me--
the camera turns on for a greeting. **

The tastiest water
all through the house
is the toilet seat bowl--
my tongue goes to douse.

It's better than frig water
and better than my bowl;
even better than rainwater
out in the backyard hole.

I drink when no one looks,
there will be no stops,
but once my human sees me
the toilet seat drops.

Yes I am a toilet cat
this is my heart's desire
but soon seats are kept down--
my water issue is dire! **

My name is Tristan
I escaped an attack
when I was very young
and could only see black.

A barn rat came
and took my family away
but somehow I escaped
away from the fray.

Some humans walked by
I meowed so faint
but they heard my cry
and became my saints.

I was taken and fixed;
since then I've been fine--
I will be fifteen soon
happiness still shines. **

My human was cleaning
off the bookshelf,
taking down books
to rearrange herself.

I saw the empty shelves
as a new cat tree
and jumped my way up
before she could see.

When she looked over
I was on the top board
she told me to get down
but I felt like a lord.

She grabbed my tail
repeating, "Get down!"
So I leaped off the shelf
giving up my crown.

The bookshelf was flimsy
with no weight from books
it began to lean down;
there were no wall hooks.

Down it collapsed
on top of the floor
book piles now scattered--
cleanup will be a chore. **

My bowl is not filled
I demand to be fed!
I will not be starved
found on the floor dead!

Fill it to the top!
Don't be stingy with food;
if you hold back
there will be a feud.

I will poop all over
and spit on the sheets;
claw at the couches
and rip up the seats.

I am the mighty cat:
hear my mew!
Hey! Don't push me away--
don't tell me to shoo! **

Socks:

Twisty ties are the best

so helpless and so cute;

I stalk them around the house

like a handsome little brute.

I carry them always

and chew them all night

once I tossed on my human--

it gave him a fright.

Then I found a whole roll

sticking out like flowers;

I tow them all over

filling up the hours.

My human was mad

finding ties everywhere;

I follow around

as he picks up my flair.

But sometimes I find one or two
and sneak away to play;
my human thinks he got them all
but I've stashed some today. **

I see a bird

calling to me--

a tasty treat

up in a tree.

I jump on branches,

starting to climb,

to get close enough

and commit my crime.

Just within range

I take my leap

but I'd misjudged--

it was too steep.

I fell to the ground

while the bird tweeted;

it looked down happy

but I felt cheated.

Before trying again
the bird flew far away;
now I stick to crickets
to toss around and play. **

My name is Gumbo
and I collect stuff;
on my nightly house prowls
I never get enough.

I dump my finds
in my water dish
they float lazily
like odd-looking fish.

My humans hide things
for me at night;
I gladly go hunting--
I never need a light.

In the morning they are happy
with my water filled so neat,
I enjoy their laughs and comments
and then I start to eat. **

I love her so much
that I purr in her ear
and tell of my love;
saying she is a dear.

She tells me to scram
so that she may sleep;
I feel like I'm a fraud--
that my love is too cheap.

I tug at her hair
to show more of my love
and mew in her face;
her nose I push and shove.

She gently pushes me off
saying she's getting up soon
but I have no issues--
I sometimes sleep 'til noon.

So I jump and bite her ears

to show my devotion;

she'll love me back I'm sure;

I don't need a love potion. **

My name is Zora
and I mew with my toys,
carrying them around
making that cute little noise.

I walk around proud
with the things I find
to let my humans know
I leave nothing behind.

One time I was mewing
and my human didn't see
I had caught a flying thing
and it wasn't a bee!

A fly flew out of my mouth
and sped away from me!
I will catch and carry anything;
I carry all I see! **

Today something happened:
we went for a car ride;
I didn't want to go--
under sheets I tried to hide.

I knew something was up;
I thought I hid myself well,
but my tail was sticking out
and became a tattletale.

Now I'm in a harness
to be taken to the car
my human comes to get me--
I'm sure this'll leave a scar.

I'm buckled in the seat
and away we go
until down the road
when vomit starts to flow. **

I have my own cat bed
but I much prefer the dog's;
I can stretch out all twisty
then start sawing logs.

The dog looks at me
and politely whines to move;
like I'd ever give this up
now that I'm in the groove.

My human tries to shoo me
but I always come back;
she crosses her arms
giving me much flack.

But I go where I please
and lay where I want
that dog can sit elsewhere
watching me flaunt. **

My human makes delicious food
but does not share with me;
I think this is unfair--
"Please give me some," I plea.

Today pancakes look delicious,
they would be a great score,
but he's always so protective
even though sometimes he gets more.

I sit quiet on the floor
waiting for the time
when he leaves the table--
that's my cue to climb.

Soon the phone distracts
and he walks away
now the pancakes are defenseless--
on the table they won't stay.

I bite into a pancake
as my human comes back;
he hauls me off the table--
I am given no slack.

Yet I always remember
that yummy pancake;
syrup melting in my mouth--
more I plan to take. **

I was curious

about those twinkling lights

wrapped around the tree

to give it some brights.

I found the rest

hidden in a box

and carry to my secret place

covered in socks.

There I got tangled up

with all the pretty lights

and walked around the house that way--

I was really a sight!

The child plugged me in

and now I am lit;

I walk next to the tree

mewing as I sit.

Now there are two things

pretty with light;

everyone laughs

as we light up the night. **

My name is Kiki
and I'm a smart little cat
who can turn on bathtub faucets--
the water falls with a splat!

It was very entertaining
to see water gushing out
I'd paw at the liquid
sniffing with my snout.

When I first turned it on
no one was around;
I stared at the blue
listening to the sound.

The water got higher
as the bathtub filled up;
I stirred my paws in it--
my very own big cup.

Then my human came in
and screeched in a fright;
they turned off the water
taking away my delight. **

There once was a bird
outside on the ground
who mocked me all the time--
it got me pretty wound.

I heard it chirping through blinds
that covered my view;
this made me irritated--
I started to stew.

I jump into the blinds
bending them round;
as I wriggle through
they make a crackling sound.

I finally see the bird!
I start mewing at it;
then my human comes in
and calls me a twit. **

Of all plants in the house
the fake one is the best;
to chew on its leaves
and put branches to the test.

I sometimes knock it down
and tug across the floor
stuffing it under the couch
to hide my awesome score.

My human catches me
saying I'm a bad kitty;
but always in the evenings
she tells me I'm pretty. **

Behold a hiking kitty!
I love to climb on rocks
and jump between the cracks;
it's better than a box.

Sometimes I get tired
and ride my human's shoulders
to take in the sights
as he walks around boulders.

The sunsets are beautiful
the wind so crisp and clear
it's amazing to be outside
and listen to all I hear.

Then we go back
to settle in for the night;
I dream about tomorrow
and of beauty that takes flight. **

My name is Alex
and I have a peculiar tic:
I keep my tail in water--
yes I'm really slick.

My human thinks I'm nuts
and moves the water bowl
But I just move with it;
I feel this in my soul.

I put my tail back
to get it nice and wet
then go back to eating;
now I am all set.

This is my peculiar tic,
my comfort while I eat;
even though I get called weird
I still get all the treats! **

I like to be up high

so I climbed onto the roof

to survey my kingdom--

I'm much more than a floof.

I could see birds

high in the trees;

plump meals chirping

but of course they're a tease.

After staring at clouds

I found

there wasn't much to do--

eh, I just want back on the ground.

I mew for my human

to come get me off;

he hears my cries

and starts to scoff.

But he brings the ladder

and carries me down

yes, we both know our place--

I wear the crown. **

The best thing to do
when my human is cleaning
is to sit by her side
nonchalantly leaning.

I look so innocent
as she unloads the dryer;
she tells me to stay
but I still watch the attire.

In the basket they go
then brought to the room
she walks away--
my mischievousness blooms.

I jump onto the clothes
and enjoy getting warm
getting cat hair all over
like a big giant swarm.

My human comes back

and gives me some talks;

she pushed me away;

fine, I'll run off with socks. **

I love to be petted;

I'm addicted I say

to being rubbed and scratched

and cuddled with all day.

If you are napping

I will wake you to scratch,

to feel fingers brush my fur--

because I am a catch.

If watching T.V.

I'll start mewing at you

to get your attention;

I'll still sing if you shoo.

I will also climb a fence

to be petted at last;

even jump in the shower--

you don't need to ask. **

I do not like change
even in tiny bits
especially small humans;
some can be twits.

They toddle around
and mess up my bed;
I hissed at one creature
to bring fear and dread.

But to my surprise
it looked at me
and hissed in my face
causing me to flee.

Now a truce is invoked
as small humans walk around:
we don't mess with each other
causing neither to frown. **

Under covers I tunnel
to slink through the sheets
exploring the darkness
sometimes finding treats.

I weave between humans
sleeping away,
wiggling through fabric
finding my way.

I peak out from under
to find them still asleep;
I don't make a sound
moving forward to creep.

I get close to a face
all relaxed and unaware;
I get even closer--
she doesn't sense my stare.

I begin to lick her nose

getting it all wet

then nibble on an ear;

I haven't been caught yet. **

I am a good kitty
most of the time
but occasionally take off
with what I consider mine.

I like to take undies
and drag across the floor
then dump in my water bowl--
ah yes, a big score.

Sometimes I take keys,
their jingle is so cute,
but my humans call me names--
they don't think it's a hoot.

One time I took homework
and played with my claws;
that's when they took treats
and laid down some laws. **

My name is Penny
and I love bottle caps.
I push them across the floor;
with my playthings I do laps.

They clang across the tile
like scattered little bugs;
they jump into clothing
and get bunched up in the rugs.

I play at night mostly
waking my human up with clatter,
she finds me having fun
then scares me away--I scatter.

She picks up my bottle caps
and throws them in the trash;
but I don't fret too much—
there will be more in a flash. **

I like the black snake
that charges the phone;
I chew on it at night
to get in the zone.

I've chewed so much
it looks frayed in most places
but I've never been caught;
never woken sleeping faces.

Until it stopped working
that's when it was found
I chewed on the snake:
no more charging sound.

Now it is covered
so I chew on some socks
but I have a secret:
the rest are kept in a box. **

I'm fascinated by the glasses
that my human wears;
I try to run off with them
but he never shares.

Sleep is the best time
to snatch them off his face
and carry them
to a secret hiding place.

Of course he wakes up
and chases me around
as I take off with the glasses
making a chirping sound.

I don't know why he doesn't share--
about them I stay curious;
yet every time I take them though
he gets a little furious. **

Elsa and Socks:

He likes to play video games
instead of petting us
so we observed his ritual--
there would be no fuss.

We began to notice
the eject button's power
stopping the game
and allowing my human to shower.

Once we learned this secret,
our plan was set in motion
we would get his attention;
we would be his only notion.

Now when he games
we sit next to that console
and play with the button
taking all the control.

My human gets mad
when we press eject;
his game isn't saved--
he usually doesn't check.

Then we mew for attention
demanding to be petted;
alas, we are ignored--
now toilet paper gets shredded. **

Elsa

Author's Note

Way back in the day I used to write poetry all the time. A few months ago I found the files on my computer and thought they were actually pretty good. So I brushed off my poetry skills and wrote about one of my favorite subjects: cats.

Elsa and Socks are my current kitties; they are such a hoot. I love their antics and how they snuggle with each other. Cat person for life.

I hope this book has brightened your day and given you a laugh.

If you are so inclined, please leave a review for this book. Reviews are very helpful to authors and much appreciated.

I am somewhat of an eclectic writer. M.G. Rorai is the pen name for my "light and breezy" works. Feel free to visit my author website, www.MGSpear.com to read my blog and subscribe for future releases.

For my "dark and brooding" stories I write under M.G. Spear.

The plan is to write more cat poetry in the future—do you want to be a part of it? If you've got a funny story or two you'd like to share, email it to meowycatstories@gmail.com. While I may not be able to personally respond to everyone, I will open them all and see what cute poems I can weave with your stories.

I look forward to sharing more works with you :).

Printed in Great Britain
by Amazon